Irish
Farmers

Ciara Ryan

St. Martin's Griffin ✹ New York

Production Manager: Adriana Coada

The Library of Congress Cataloging-in-Publication Data is available upon request.

ISBN 978-1-250-08876-5 (trade paperback)
ISBN 978-1-250-08877-2 (e-book)

Our books may be purchased in bulk for promotional, educational, or business use. Please contact your local bookseller or the Macmillan Corporate and Premium Sales Department at (800) 221-7945, extension 5442, or by e-mail at MacmillanSpecialMarkets@macmillan.com.

First Edition: March 2016

10 9 8 7 6 5 4 3 2 1

To the farmers

acknowledgments

I wish to thank Sorche Fairbank from Fairbank Literary Representation for her unwavering belief in the Irish Farmer. For being a wonderful support throughout the making of this book, much love and gratitude. A big thank you Daniela Rapp, Lauren Jablonski, and all the team at St. Martin's Press for their amazing efforts and creativity in all areas of production.

It all started with a charity-based calendar. The Irish Farmer calendar series commenced in 2010. After observing the popularity of the Fire Fighter's calendar, both in New York and a subsequent Irish edition, I realized the farmer was a great Irish icon and yet they weren't being represented. I set about to change that. When our search for farmers commenced in 2009, I wanted to make a calendar that contained 100 percent Irish Beef, genuine farmers with farmers tans, no fake bake, and no makeup. This had to be the real deal, and of course it had to be humorous and little "out there." And it was important to all of us to make this mean something, so we chose to support Bóthar, an Irish charity that enables families and communities worldwide to overcome hunger and poverty and to restore the environment in a sustainable way. The charity specializes in improved livestock production and supports related training and community development. Bóthar also educates the public about global poverty. Bóthar benefitted from sales of the calendar. The book you're holding also helps to support Bóthar.

The first calendar was a huge online success, both in Ireland and abroad, and as a result, we decided to continue into 2011 in the hopes that this quirky catalogue of topless men was not a one-hit-wonder. Now, heading into 2016, we have just completed our seventh calendar and are amazed with the series' popularity and the loyalty of our fans throughout the years. It must be noted that the calendar was not a one-woman show and many wonderful people made it possible over the years through hard work, a great attitude, a broad mind, and a boatload of creativity.

With this is mind, I wish to thank Dominic at Castlewood Farm for pulling out all the stops, to Charlotte and Kevina at Glendeer Pet Farm, and to Deirdre at Causey Farm. Special thanks to Jeanne from Brooke Cottage for "heaven on earth." Thanks to Pat McCarrick at Bóthar for being an absolute gentleman. To Kevin and all the team at Pigsback.com, many thanks. Deep gratitude to Gareth Alcorn, George Smyth, Keiran Nipress, and all the team at Nore Valley Park who went above and beyond for us—much love. To Steve at Precision Print for his great patience and understanding. To our wonderful photographers David Kenna, Tom Morgan, Ian Shipley, Frances Marshall, and Jan Golden for producing such amazing, quirky pictures and being a joy to work with. And finally, a massive thank-you to the stars of the show, the Irish Farmers, who signed up for the calendar series, without knowing what sort of position they'd be put in, what animal they'd be posing with, and what slagging they would get in the aftermath. The lovely lads never regretted taking part and some even signed up again in subsequent years for more punishment! Without you, none of this would be possible. Thank you!

Irish
Farmers

GARETH

I'm a qualified adventure-sports instructor for rock climbing, paddling, mountain biking, and skiing.

JAN

I had a pet peeve once, but he was run over by a tractor.

JAMIE

I can crack an egg with no hands.

My dream job? A male stripper.

I was letting the chickens out one morning and the geese, who hate me, spotted that I was cornered and decided to have a go at me. Me being the "athlete" I think I am, ran and jumped over them. Unfortunately I did not escape unharmed as one of the sneaky bastards managed to bite my meat and two veg.

What moment of the photo shoot are you glad did not get captured? When I was getting my makeup done.

Interesting Farmer Fact: Jamie is Gary's son.

GARY

What is the funniest thing that ever happened to you in connection with livestock? I was removing rope that had been caught up round the blades of a grass mower, on my knees cutting away with a knife, when Timothy, a huge texel ram decided it was his opportunity to, let's say get a bit friendly. He jumped me from the rear pinning me to the mower. I called the wife to get him off, she called back "Now ya know what it feels like, darling."

JOHN W.

JOHN R.

JOHN F.

The worst stereotype about farmers ever is that we are all old and wear tweed and wellies and stand around talking about the war or something. During the harvest I'd be sitting in the harvester in shorts and vest top with my Ray-Bans on listening to the latest tunes.

I can play the spoons to two national anthems.

EOIN

STEPHEN

My perfect date is a female version of me!

AODHGAN

I HAVE A BLACK CAT
CALLED TEAPOT. HE
HAS A GOOD SENSE OF
HUMOR.

RICHARD

I'm a great man to boil an egg.

If I was cooking dinner and I could invite anybody, it would be the Marx Brothers.

PAUL

STEPHEN

My least favorite animal is the Loch Ness monster.

THE WORST
STEREOTYPE
ABOUT FARMERS?
THEY ARE ALL
TRUE.

JAN

My favorite way to spend a Saturday is outdoors, talking to my trees while grooming them.

I never have farming nightmares, the sixteen pints before bed means no dreams.

I almost became a Chinese medical practitioner, but decided on farming instead.

COLM

DARRAGH

Repairing things is not a talent I was blessed with.
But when it comes to breaking things, I'm an expert.

KEVIN

Favorite food and where to eat it? Hang sangiches and tae with a slice of apple tart, best served in the cab of my tractor, late evening during silage season! Mammy's lasagne is pretty good, too.

How did you become a farmer? Well sure yer born into it aren't ya! You don't pick it, it picks you! It's more of a vocation, bit like joining the priests, but with more tits!

My least favorite animal is our sheepdog. He's shite, so shite we didn't even name him, he's just called Dog.

DAVID

I AM A
NO-NONSENSE
FARMER.

PATRICK

The best phrase in Gaelic is *An bhfuil cead agam dul go dtí an leithreas*, which means: "The love you give to an animal in life echoes through the generations." (It actually means "Can I go to the toilet.")

My perfect date? Just me (no shirt), hay, a nice evening, and chewing the cud with my animals

Cows' arses make me laugh.

MICHAEL

LEO

I am a sheep whisperer.

Sing to your cows, they love it

GARETH

I had a nightmare once that the cows ran the farm and starting milking me.

Almost became a detective, but decided on farming instead.

My pet deer Stanley is my favorite animal. He is the first one I ever hand-reared and he is still super friendly with me, he always comes over for a hug!

I can drink a pint of Guinness in three
seconds (DON'T TELL MY MAMMY!).

I'm glad they didn't take a photo of me when
I wasn't sucking it in!

BARRY

I feel that Irish farmers have been misrepresented.

My favorite place in Ireland is on the Boyne River. One time a herd of cows congregated and stared at me across the river. It's magical.

My only requirement for a girlfriend is that she bring her own wellies.

The best phrase in Gaelic is *An miste leat labhairt níos moille?* It means: "Can you speak a little slower?"

JAMES

I HAVE TWO
PET PIGS
CALLED
CHEESE AND
ONION.

JOHN F.

When machinery breaks down or things
start going wrong I use an awful lot of curse
words. They can consist of "feck," "dirty dog,"
"well that's put the straw hat on it now."

STEPHEN

I'm very partial to afternoon delight, be it swimming, spending time with friends, or enjoying nature.

Secret farming tip: A bottle of stout can stop a cow coughing.

GEAROID

The best phrase in Gaelic is *Pog mo thoin*, "Kiss my ass."

What can you repair? A broken heart.

What animal scares you? Females.

I am happy being a beef farmer as I haven't the patience to look at four tits morning and evening milking cows.

PAUL

DAVID

All you need to fix anything that's broke is a hammer, vice grips, insulating tape, and WD-40; all other tools are a waste of money. If they can't do it, it's definitely fucked.

Do you have a dream job besides farming?
I'd love to be a console games tester.

GARETH

If you were cooking dinner and you could invite anybody, dead or alive, famous or not; who would you invite? Probably an unusual choice, but Genghis Khan. I read a book about his life and what he achieved in life blew me away.

MARK

I used to have a dog and cats as pets. Now I have a snail on the wall in my shower room. I've called him Trevor. (I'm not sure how to tell the sex of a snail so I've just taken the risk of assuming it's male.) He's a good listener and loves my singing in the shower.

I was once back-kicked by a cow in my "man parts." And I swear to this day that cow had a smile on her face. I had just called her a "fat cow" so this may be described as karma.

ANIMALS NEVER DO
WHAT YOU WANT
THEM TO.

DAVID

My perfect date is a long walk on a short beach.

I almost became a boring person, but decided on farming instead.

JOHN W.

CONOR

JOHN F.

My best farming story is probably one day I was spreading cow slurry and the back got blocked. Forgetting to close the back valve, I started releasing the blockage. When I released it, the pressure behind it was unreal and covered me head to toe in cow waste. I had to walk home and hose myself down in the yard. I smelled rotten for a week but had no problem getting a spot at the bar.

I WOULD LOVE
TO BE THE
NEXT WOLF OF
WALL STREET.

DONAGH

I almost became a professional rugby player, but decided on farming instead.

STEPHEN

I almost became a priest, but decided on farming instead.

GEORGE

THERE HAS GOT TO BE MORE TO LIFE THAN THIS SHIT!

JASON

ANDREW

GERARD

CONOR

Perfect date: Latin dancing.

My favorite Irish quote is: "Life's too short not to be Irish." *Tá saol a gheart san a bheith Èireannach.*

JOHN F.

Ryan Reynolds would have to play me in the
Irish Farmers movie.

CARLOS

ANIMALS
ARE BETTER
LISTENERS.

CHARLIE

What sort of farmer are you? A bad one.

Describe your perfect date: Someone comfortable enough with themselves and not an arse.

What do you look for in a mate? Nothing. Looking for stuff spoils the real stuff.

If you could be a different kind of farmer, what would you farm? Money trees.

Do you have a dream job besides farming? Rockstar.

The most memorable moment about the photo shoot? Oh Jaysus!!!!! The duck took a poo on me . . . in the bath . . . while in my hands.

CONOR

ANDREW

TERRY

Worst stereotype about farmers?
Farmer's tan.

CARLOS

OH JAYSUS, HERE WE GO!

GER

BRENDAN

SHEEP AND RAMS
SCARE ME! THEY
ARE THE SILENT
JUDGMENTAL
ANIMALS.

JOHN

Do you have any pet peeves? Bad grammar.

What do you look for in a spouse? I am happily engaged to my future husband, so he is perfect in every way.

Always walk on rushes in marshy land. . . . You are less likely to lose your Wellingtons this way!

KIERAN

I am the best stone picker in Ireland!!

Always watch yourself, especially around livestock! Don't turn your back.

TREVOR

DAVID

GER

GEORGE

All farmers enjoy the peace and crackle of a fire.

I get annoyed when people take a shower and leave water on the floor after it.

PAUL

I THINK PEOPLE THINK ALL FARMERS "DO IT" IN THEIR WELLIES. THAT'S NOT TRUE, IT'S ONLY SOME OF US.

MARK

I love to be active so a perfect Saturday would be to get up early, go for a cross-country run or work out in the gym, maybe a swim in the lake nearby. Then I like to explore new places so maybe a trip out in the car to somewhere I can take a walk and investigate historical sites, art galleries, science shows. To end a Saturday, I like nothing better than to light the fire, put on a film, and eat my body weight in chocolate. . . .

My perfect date would actually be the stereotypical "roll in the hay" (it's a farmer thing . . . what can I say?). I like to be with someone who is very active and enjoys the outdoors. So maybe a picnic would be a good date. No frills, no pretense, just two people and the great outdoors . . . oh . . . and maybe a flask of luke warm tea and an egg-and-onion sandwich. Ya can't have a picnic without them!

BRENDAN

What do you look for in a mate? Road frontage.

Best word or phrase in Gaelic? *Ta tu chomh mistumaigh le muic I mala.* "You are as awkward as a pig in a sack."

BARRY AODHGAN DECLAN

STEPHEN   JASON   GARETH   GEORGE   KIERAN   ANDREW

ANDREW

I am twenty-five (or 307 months as the pre-ferred method for telling the age of a cow).

Describe your perfect date: That's a tough one. I'd have to say April 25th. Because it's not too hot, not too cold, all you need is a light jacket.

What do you look for in a mate? I've found her already, golden blonde hair, she never gives out, great listener, and she'll come with me in the tractor and loves getting her paws dirty. You're on about my golden Labrador, right?

I can juggle. I am a wizard at reversing a trailer. I come from one of the most inland counties in Ireland and I surf.

GEORGE

One memory of the photo shoot that stood out was when one of the farmers had to get a picture with a goat eating from between the farmer's legs. Let's just say that the goat got a bit adventurous.

I love building LEGO Technic and I am always seeking my next project.

I wish folks who are not in the biz knew the difference between straw and hay. I teach about one thousand people the difference between both each year. Need a parrot to repeat it for me at this stage.

I do organic farming in County Mayo, in Ireland's northwest, but I am also a reggae recording artist.

KIERAN

What do you look for in a mate? Living and willing.

If you could be a different kind of farmer, what would you farm? Crops I suppose—they stay in the field and don't wander or run off on ya.

What did/does your mum most often say about you? You're covered in muck and clean your boots.

DAVID

CIARÁN

A pet peeve is a challenge you won't conquer.

If I were cooking dinner and you could invite anybody, it would have to be Bruce Lee, Socrates, and Jean-Luc Picard.

Favorite food and where to eat it? Porridge and raspberries in the bedroom.

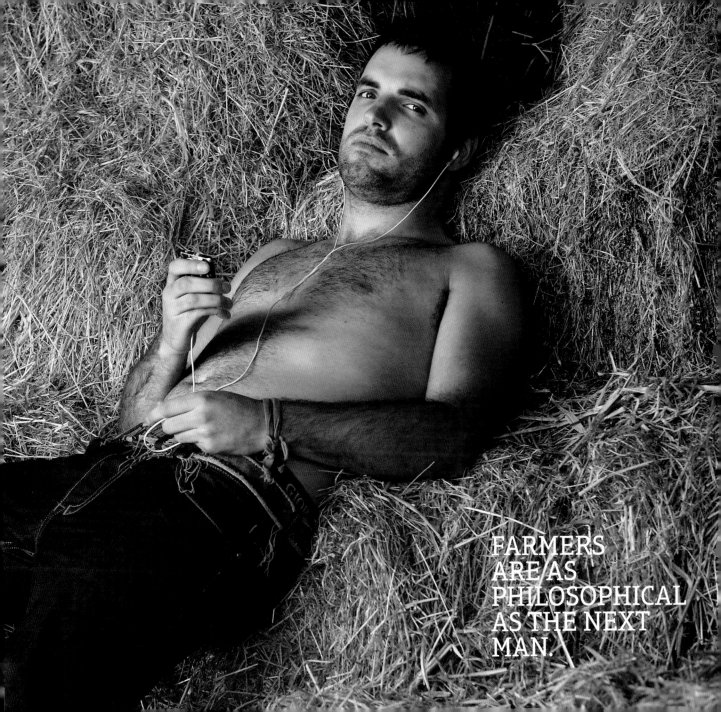

FARMERS
ARE AS
PHILOSOPHICAL
AS THE NEXT
MAN.

JASON

KYLE

DONAGH

DAVID ANDREW JAMES

MICHAEL

COLIN

You can't beat a traditional meal of spuds, bacon, and cabbage!

I almost became a carpenter, but decided on farming instead.

DECLAN

PADDY

What do you look for in a mate? Eyesight, if she's fully able to see and still fancies me it's a great start!

I can drive a tractor with just my knees although I'm sure there's a law against that.

An ounce of breeding is worth a ton of feeding.

I'm awful clever; it's a bit of a burden really.

I almost became a normal person, but decided on farming instead.